D1476872

Published in 2018 by The Rosen Publishing Group, Inc.
29 East 21st Street, New York, NY 10010

Editor: Elizabeth Krajnik
Book Design: Michael Flynn
Interior Layout: Tanya Dellaccio

Photo Credits: Cover, pp. 11, 13 Nativestock.com/Marilyn Angel Wynn/Nativestock/Getty Images; p. 5 Bildagentur Zoonar GmbH/Shutterstock.com; p. 6 DAVID MCNEW/AFP/Getty Images; p. 7 Richard PJ Lambert/Moment/Getty Images; p. 9 Luz-i/Shutterstock.com; p. 10 GUDKOV ANDREY/Shutterstock.com; p. 15 Marilyn Angel Wynn/Nativestock/Getty Images; p. 17 Florilegius/SSPL/Getty Images; p. 19 moosehenderson/Shutterstock.com; pp. 21, 27 DEA/G. DAGLI ORTI/De Agostini/Getty Images; pp. 22, 24 Courtesy of the Library of Congress; p. 23 https://commons.wikimedia.org/wiki/File:Carlos_III_cazador.jpg; p. 25 Glenn W. Walker/Shutterstock.com; p. 29 Courtesy of the New York Public Library Digital Collections.

Library of Congress Cataloging-in-Publication Data

Names: Mendoza, Charlie, 1982- author.
Title: The Ohlone / Charlie Mendoza.
Description: New York : PowerKids Press, 2018. | Series: Spotlight on the
  American Indians of California | Includes index.
Identifiers: LCCN 2017024172| ISBN 9781538324837 (library bound) | ISBN
  9781538324868 (pbk.) | ISBN 9781538324875 (6 pack)
Subjects: LCSH: Ohlone Indians--California--History--Juvenile literature. |
  Ohlone Indians--California--Social life and customs--Juvenile literature.
Classification: LCC E99.C8744 M46 2018 | DDC 979.4004/97--dc23
LC record available at https://lccn.loc.gov/2017024172

Manufactured in China

CPSIA Compliance Information: Batch #BW18PK For further information contact Rosen Publishing, New York, New York at 1-800-237-9932.

CONTENTS

CHAPTER ONE

OHLONE COUNTRY

The lands between San Francisco Bay and Monterey Bay in California were once home to a group of American Indians known today as the Ohlone people. There, the Ohlone people built an amazing culture that allowed them to **prosper** for more than a thousand years.

Anthropologists and other experts estimate that the Ohlones' **ancestors** arrived in North America between 40,000 and 13,000 years ago. Over many thousands of years, the ancestors of the Ohlones moved south into what is now central California.

The Ohlones identified themselves not as members of one big group but rather according to what community they were from. The name "Ohlone" came into use in the late 20th century. The origin of this name is unknown. Previously, members of the Ohlone nations were called Costanoans, a name given to them by Spanish settlers.

Some scholars and American Indians believe the Ohlones are descendants of the first American Indian groups to live in central California. They believe the Ohlones have always lived in the areas where they were found by the Spaniards in 1769.

CHAPTER TWO

USING WHAT THEY HAD

The Ohlones depended very heavily on what the earth had to offer. They found **abundant** sources of food in the plants that grew in the area. The Ohlones harvested dozens of plants and plant items, including grasses and nuts. Their lands also provided many kinds of game.

Every year, the Ohlone people burned the open spaces that surrounded the trees in their community's forests. This action increased the amount of food that the

The Ohlones depended on many different kinds of stones and **minerals**. Salt, which was collected from salt ponds like the ones pictured here in San Francisco, was an important item in everyone's diet.

land would produce by making it easier for wild grasses and flowers to grow. These plants produced seeds that served as food for the Ohlones and many of the animals they hunted.

Rocks were necessary for the creation of many of the basic tools the Ohlones used every day. Wood from trees was carved into hundreds of kinds of tools, such as bows, spears, knife handles, and paddles.

CHAPTER THREE

GETTING CRAFTY

The Ohlones created jewelry and tools from raw materials found around them. Nearly all American Indian groups depended on stone as one of their most important resources. The Ohlones ground harder types of rocks into many different forms. They also created arrowheads, knives, and other objects by chipping stone.

Parts from the animals the Ohlones hunted were also used to create tools and jewelry. Bones were made into beads, earrings, musical instruments, and tools. Turtle shells and deer hooves were transformed into rattles. Sinew, a kind of muscle, was removed from the bodies of deer and combined with wood to make powerful bows.

Plants provided another important source for raw materials. The Ohlones frequently navigated the coastal areas using reed canoes called *tule balsas*. Each canoe was about 10 feet (3 m) long and 3 feet (1 m) wide.

These Argentinian *boleadoras* look similar to the bolas the Ohlones used to hunt. When thrown into the air, the bola twisted. It could easily knock a bird out of the sky and trip a running animal.

CHAPTER FOUR

MAKING MEALS

The Ohlones prepared their meals in a number of ways. They cooked many items by roasting them over an open flame. Other foods were steamed or smoked over slow-burning fires.

Some meals were prepared in pit ovens, which were large holes dug into the ground. A fire was built in each pit. Stones were slowly added to the flames. When the rocks were red hot, poles were used to drag the

The Ohlones did not use pottery or stone bowls for cooking. Instead, they prepared stews and similar dishes using tightly woven baskets.

rocks out of the pit. Some of the rocks were put back into the hole along with foods such as shellfish or meat wrapped in leaves. Additional hot rocks were piled on top. After a few hours, the food was ready.

Many of the Ohlones' foods were only available during certain seasons. Some things could be preserved for later use. The plants that were gathered could be dried in the sun.

CHAPTER FIVE

LIVING TOGETHER

Like many other American Indian groups living in California, the Ohlones always built their villages near flowing water. These villages varied in size. Some had as few as 50 people, while others may have had as many as 500 people.

The Ohlones lived in small huts made of poles, grass, or reeds. The huts had circular floor plans and ranged from 6 to 20 feet (1.8 to 6.1 m) wide. People slept on reed mats or blankets next to the walls. In the center of each hut was a fire pit used for heat and cooking. One or two related families occupied each dwelling.

Most Ohlone villages also included a single larger home that was reserved for the use of the chief, or community leader. Around 200 people could fit inside this building.

The Ohlones moved around to find more natural resources. They built temporary villages at new harvesting sites. Their settlements were easy to build, so the frequent movement of the communities didn't make too much extra work.

CHAPTER SIX

OHLONE FASHION

California's weather allowed the Ohlone people to go without much clothing for most of the year. Men and children usually wore no clothing at all. When it was cold or wet, the Ohlones wore robes, short capes, or blankets. Sometimes, the men covered their bodies with mud to protect them from the cold.

Unlike many other American Indian groups, the Ohlone men often wore beards and mustaches. Their hair was usually worn in braids or tied up in the back. The women wore more clothing than the men. Every adult female had a two-piece skirt. Ohlone women also had **tattoos** that indicated where they grew up. Their long hair usually fell over their shoulders.

Both men and women enjoyed wearing jewelry, including bracelets and beads. They also combined a number of materials to create paints they used to decorate their bodies.

The Ohlone wore body paint for **ceremonies**, warfare, and hunting. The most common colors were black, white, red, and brown. Many villages had their own sets of symbols that residents painted on their bodies.

CHAPTER SEVEN

OHLONE TRADITIONS AND RELIGION

The Ohlone people believed that natural resources, such as the plants they ate and water they drank, were alive and had to be treated with respect. When they used something, they often said a special prayer. They believed that they had to balance their needs with those of other kinds of life.

During celebrations and **rituals**, the Ohlones wore beautiful headpieces, skirts, and feather cloaks and robes. Some Ohlone villages had oval dance enclosures. Many of the places where the Ohlones lived and worked were also seen as sacred places. They often planted prayer sticks decorated with feathers at these locations and treated them with special respect.

Most Ohlone holidays and celebrations were connected to their religion. Their daily life was filled with rituals that marked the journey a person makes from birth to death, as well as the changing seasons.

Ohlone religious celebrations often featured dances that included imitations of animals. Some of these songs and dances are still performed today.

The Ohlones had a **complex** set of beliefs that provided them with a way to understand the universe and all that it contained. They believed the story of their people started with a coyote, an eagle, and a hummingbird. Together, these three creatures made the human race. Some elders thought this origin was why the Ohlone clans were connected to the animal world.

The northern Ohlones usually burned their dead. In the south, only the bodies of the most important people were burned; everyone else was buried. The ashes or other remains were buried near their villages. Ohlone religion prevented the people from talking about the dead or even mentioning their names.

Both men and women could become spiritual leaders. They knew many special rituals, dances, and songs. The spiritual leaders were always respected and sometimes feared.

Each Ohlone village had a sweat lodge, which was mainly used by men. Inside the sweat lodge, the men used the heat for cleansing and healing. Sometimes they sang special songs while they were inside.

CHAPTER EIGHT

SOCIAL STRUCTURE

Ohlone individuals were assigned to a group based on how old they were, where they were born, whether they were men or women, and who their father was. The smallest Ohlone social unit was the family. The work that each family member was assigned was usually determined by the person's age and if they were male or female.

Ohlone families were combined into larger groups called clans. Every clan had certain religious responsibilities. The clans were further grouped into larger units called moieties. The moieties had specific ceremonial jobs members did to make sure the Ohlone nation was healthy and successful.

The position of chief was handed down from father to son. A council of village elders aided the chief. The chiefs were given special privileges. They organized religious ceremonies, provided **hospitality** to visitors, and led the people during times of trouble.

This image created by Louis Choris in 1822 shows Ohlone men fishing in a *tule balsa* near San Francisco.

CHAPTER NINE

EUROPEAN EXPLORATION

Much of what we know about the Ohlones' history comes from records kept by European explorers. In 1602, Sebastian Vizcaíno became the first European explorer to make contact with the Ohlone people. Between 1602 and 1769, other explorers and Spanish merchant ships sometimes stopped on the coast. While these explorers'

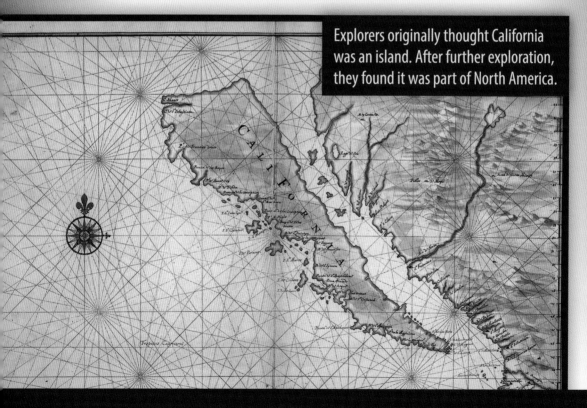

Explorers originally thought California was an island. After further exploration, they found it was part of North America.

KING CARLOS III

aims may have been good, they accidentally introduced horrible diseases that may have killed as much as 95 percent of American Indian populations.

King Carlos III of Spain believed he had the right to send soldiers to take over anything he wanted within the California American Indians' homeland. During the middle of the 18th century, the king became concerned about English and Russian exploration of the Pacific coast. He was afraid they would send troops and ships to take over "his" territory.

CHAPTER TEN

THE OHLONES AND THE SPANISH MISSIONS

In 1769, King Carlos III launched an expedition to take control of California. The next year, the capital of Spain's new **province** was established near Monterey Bay. The outpost included a military base and a kind of religious settlement called a mission.

Spain's leaders built missions with the goal of making the American Indians citizens of Spain. King Carlos III chose a group of priests headed by Junípero Serra to undertake this task. These priests,

Mission San Francisco de Asís, or Mission Dolores, was founded October 9, 1776. The original mission building survived the San Francisco earthquake of 1906 and is one of the oldest standing buildings in San Francisco.

MISSION DOLORES

called missionaries, thought they could improve the lives of the American Indians by providing them with advanced **technology** and new plants and animals.

The missionaries' goal was to build a community for God that would improve the futures of the Spaniards and the American Indians. Between 1770 and 1835, seven missions were built for the Ohlones.

CHAPTER ELEVEN

THE OHLONES JOIN THE MISSIONS

The success of the missions depended on the willingness of the Ohlones and other American Indians to join them. The missionaries persuaded the Ohlone people with promises of help during wartime. The Spaniards brought powerful weapons, such as firearms and steel swords.

The missionaries reached out to the Ohlones, many of whom decided to move to the missions as neophytes, or new followers. The village chiefs sometimes brought their whole communities to the missions. Once they had moved, these elders often continued to serve as leaders. The neophytes sometimes persuaded their relatives, whom the missionaries called gentiles, to come live with them at the mission.

Many Ohlones rejected the missions. Those who lived away from the missions often felt threatened by the new communities. To them, the creation of the missions was the same thing as a declaration of war. This lead to fighting between the two groups.

The Spanish often enslaved American Indians who resisted moving to the missions. This engraving by Louis Choris shows American Indians forced to work at the military base in San Francisco.

27

CHAPTER TWELVE

THE END OF THE MISSION ERA

In 1822, Mexico gained control of California and the Ohlones became Mexican citizens. However, they weren't treated the same as other Mexican citizens. The Ohlones and other American Indians were promised rights but never received them. Some were even captured and enslaved.

Some of the former neophytes escaped to the east and joined other American Indian peoples. They helped organize surprise attacks that captured thousands of cattle and horses from Mexican ranches. By 1845, it looked as if the American Indians might drive the newcomers out of California.

However, everything changed in 1848 when California became part of the United States as a result of the U.S.-Mexican War. Soon, the gold rush brought tens of thousands of newcomers to California. The remaining lands that once belonged to American Indians were quickly occupied without regard to the previous owners.

In 1850, the governor of California ordered a war of **extermination** against the remaining American Indians. New laws made it possible for government officials to imprison poor American Indians and make them work for free.

CHAPTER THIRTEEN

THE OHLONE PEOPLE TODAY

To protect themselves, many American Indians claimed they were Mexicans. Mexicans were treated better than American Indians were. The tiny communities of traditional Ohlone people that remained barely survived into the 20th century. They struggled to protect their civil rights and rebuild their culture. In 1924, all American Indians were granted U.S. citizenship. By this time, very few Ohlones could speak their native language.

Many Ohlones have preserved their identity as American Indians. It's uncertain how many people belong to the Ohlone nation today. However, a number of Ohlone groups, such as the Ohlone/Costanoan Esselen Nation of Monterey County, have been organized. Many of these groups are still fighting to be recognized by the U.S. government. The Ohlones are working to restore their traditions and continue to fight for their rights as American Indians.

GLOSSARY

abundant (uh-BUHN-duhnt) Existing in large amounts.

ancestor (AN-ses-tuhr) Someone in your family who lived long before you.

anthropologist (an-thruh-PAH-luh-jist) A scientist who studies the history and society of humans.

ceremony (SEHR-uh-moh-nee) A formal act or event that is part of a social or religious occasion.

complex (kahm-PLEHKS) Not easy to understand or explain; having many parts.

extermination (ik-stuhr-muh-NAY-shun) The act of destroying or killing a group of people completely.

hospitality (hah-spuh-TAA-luh-tee) Generous and friendly treatment of visitors and guests.

mineral (MIH-nuh-ruhl) A natural substance that is formed under the ground.

prosper (PRAHS-puhr) To become or be very successful.

province (PRAH-vuhns) Any one of the large parts some countries are divided into.

ritual (RIH-choo-uhl) A religious ceremony, especially one consisting of a series of actions performed in a certain order.

tattoo (taa-TOO) A picture or design made by putting color under the skin.

technology (tek-NAH-luh-jee) The way people do something and the tools they use.

INDEX

PRIMARY SOURCE LIST

Page 22
Map of California shown as an island. Created by Joan Vinckeboons. ca. 1650. Now kept at the Library of Congress Geography and Map Division, Washington, D.C.

Page 27
Vue du Presidio Sn. Francisco. Engraving. Created by Louis Choris. ca. 1822. Now kept at the Bancroft Library, University of California Berkeley, California.

Page 29
Protecting the Settlers. Wood engraving. Created by J. Ross Browne. Published in *Harper's Weekly*, Volume 23, 1861. Now kept at the New York Public Library Picture Collection Online.

WEBSITES

Due to the changing nature of Internet links, PowerKids Press has developed an online list of websites related to the subject of this book. This site is updated regularly. Please use this link to access the list: www.powerkidslinks.com/saic/ohl